Crochet Bright

Scarves, Hats, Booties, and More

KRISTIN SPURKLAND

Martingale®
Create with Confidence

Crochet Bright: Scarves, Hats, Booties, and More
© 2013 by Kristin Spurkland

Martingale®
19021 120th Ave. NE, Ste. 102
Bothell, WA 98011-9511 USA
ShopMartingale.com

Printed in China

18 17 16 15 14 13   8 7 6 5 4 3 2 1

Library of Congress Cataloging-in-Publication Data is available upon request.

ISBN: 978-1-60468-315-8

Mission Statement
Dedicated to providing quality products
and service to inspire creativity.

Contents

Footies

Somewhere between a sock and a slipper, these foot warmers are super cozy and much faster to crochet than a regular sock.

Sizes

To fit: 2-4 yrs (4-6 yrs, Child Large/Adult Small, Adult Medium, Adult Large, Adult Extra Large)
Foot circumference: 5½ (6½, 7½, 8½, 9½, 10¼)"
Foot length: 6 (7, 8, 9, 10, 11)"

Note: These slipper socks can be worn a bit smaller or a bit larger than your actual foot size. Made small, they will stretch to accommodate your feet and fit like socks; made large, they fit like slippers.

Materials

Yarn: 100% merino wool worsted-weight yarn (4) in following amounts:
  MC: 175 (175, 175, 350, 350, 350) yds
  CC: Small amount
Hook: Size H-8 (5 mm) crochet hook
Notions: Split-ring markers (having 2 different colors is helpful), tapestry needle, optional fabric paint or no-slip spray (available at home-improvement and hardware stores) to give soles some grip

Gauge

17 sts and 20 rnds = 4" in sc on H-8 hook

Right Foot

All sizes: With MC, ch 8. Sc in front lp of 2nd ch from hook and in next 6 chs, do not turn, sc in next 7 chs along lower edge of ch—14 sc. Pm in last st of rnd. Move marker to last st of each subsequent rnd.

Right Toe Shaping

Rnd 1: Work 3 sc in next st, sc in next 6 sts, work 3 sc in next st, sc in next 6 sts—18 sts.
Rnd 2: Sc in next st, work 3 sc in next st, sc in next 8 sts, work 3 sc in next st, sc in next 7 sts—22 sts.
Rnd 3: Sc in next 2 sts, work 3 sc in next st, sc to end of rnd—24 sts. (Size 2-4 yrs, skip to ** above right.)
Rnd 4: Sc in next 3 sts, work 3 sc in next st, sc to end of rnd—26 sts.
Rnd 5: Sc in next 4 sts, work 3 sc in next st, sc to end of rnd—28 sts. (Size 4-6 yrs, skip to ** above right.)
Rnd 6: Sc in next 5 sts, work 3 sc in next st, sc to end of rnd—30 sts.

Rnd 7: Sc in next 6 sts, work 3 sc in next st, sc to end of rnd—32 sts. (Size Child Large/Adult Small, skip to ** below.)
Rnd 8: Sc in next 7 sts, work 3 sc in next st, sc to end of rnd—34 sts.
Rnd 9: Sc in next 8 sts, work 3 sc in next st, sc to end of rnd—36 sts. (Size Adult Medium, skip to ** below.)
Rnd 10: Sc in next 9 sts, work 3 sc in next st, sc to end of rnd—38 sts.
Rnd 11: Sc in next 10 sts, work 3 sc in next st, sc to end of rnd—40 sts. (Size Adult Large, skip to ** below.)
Rnd 12: Sc in next 11 sts, work 3 sc in next st, sc to end of rnd—42 sts.
Rnd 13: Sc in next 12 sts, work 3 sc in next st, sc to end of rnd—44 sts. (Size Adult Extra Large, go to ** below.)
**Work even in sc on 24 (28, 32, 36, 40, 44) sts for 18 (20, 22, 24, 26, 28) rnds.

Mark that Spot

To keep track of increases, place the marker in the center stitch of three single crochets worked into one stitch. On the next round, the increase occurs in the stitch with the marker.

Reposition markers for foot opening: Hold slipper so that top is facing you (as if you were about to put it on). Find center-front st and mark it. It helps to put slipper on foot to confirm that marked st is at center front. Pm in 2nd (2nd, 3rd, 3rd, 4th, 4th) st to left of marked center st. This is marker A. Pm in 3rd (3rd, 4th, 4th, 5th, 5th) st to right of marked center st. This is marker B. If you have different-colored markers, use different colors for A and B so you can tell them apart. You should have 6 (6, 8, 8, 10, 10) sts marked off, centered around center-front st marker. Remove markers at center-front foot and beg of rnd; markers A and B remain.

Heel

Sc around slipper, stopping at marker A (do not work into marked st), turn.

Ch 1, sc across next 18 (22, 24, 28, 30, 34) heel sts, stopping at marker B (do not work into marked st), turn.

(Ch 1, sc across heel sts, turn) for 6 (8, 8, 10, 10, 12) rows. Break yarn. Remove markers.

Heel Flap

With RS of heel sts facing you, rejoin yarn in 6th (8th, 8th, 10th, 10th, 12th) st from end and sc across center 6 (6, 8, 8, 10, 10) heel-flap sts, turn.

(Ch 1, sc across heel-flap sts, turn) for 6 (8, 8, 10, 10, 12) rows. Break yarn.

Finishing

Sew heel-flap seams with overcast st from RS. (With yarn threaded through tapestry needle, *insert needle into BL of edge stitch from each edge to be joined, pull yarn through, rep from * to end of seam.)

Sew heel-flap seams.

Trim: Rejoin yarn at center-back heel. With MC, sc 2 rnds around foot opening; then with CC, sc 1 rnd. Finish last rnd by joining last st of rnd to first st of rnd with sl st. Break yarn and fasten off.

Weave in ends. Block footie into shape.

Twisted Footie?

Because it's worked in a long, narrow spiral, the footie will have a slight torque or twist, which will disappear as soon as the footie is put on. This shape helps the footie hug your foot more closely.

Left Foot

Work left foot as for right, reversing toe shaping as follows:

Left Toe Shaping

Rnd 1: Work 3 sc in next st, sc in next 6 sts, work 3 sc in next st, sc in next 6 sts—18 sts.

Rnd 2: Sc in next st, work 3 sc in next st, sc in next 8 sts, work 3 sc in next st, sc in next 7 sts—22 sts.

Rnd 3: Sc in next 13 sts, work 3 sc in next st, sc to end of rnd—24 sts. (Size 2–4 yrs, skip to ** on page 5.)

Rnd 4: Sc in next 14 sts, work 3 sc in next st, sc to end of rnd—26 sts.

Rnd 5: Sc in next 15 sts, work 3 sc in next st, sc to end of rnd—28 sts. (Size 4–6 yrs, skip to ** on page 5.)

Rnd 6: Sc in next 16 sts, work 3 sc in next st, sc to end of rnd—30 sts.

Rnd 7: Sc in next 17 sts, work 3 sc in next st, sc to end of rnd—32 sts. (Size Child Large/Adult Small, skip to ** on page 5.)

Rnd 8: Sc in next 18 sts, work 3 sc in next st, sc to end of rnd—34 sts.

Rnd 9: Sc in next 19 sts, work 3 sc in next st, sc to end of rnd—36 sts. (Size Adult Medium, skip to ** on page 5.)

Rnd 10: Sc in next 20 sts, work 3 sc in next st, sc to end of rnd—38 sts.

Rnd 11: Sc in next 21 sts, work 3 sc in next st, sc to end of rnd—40 sts. (Size Adult Large, skip to ** on page 5.)

Rnd 12: Sc in next 22 sts, work 3 sc in next st, sc to end of rnd—42 sts.

Rnd 13: Sc in next 23 sts, work 3 sc in next st, sc to end of rnd—44 sts. (Size Adult Extra Large, skip to ** on page 5.)

Work rem of left foot as for right foot.

Matched Set

A coordinating set of Fingerless Mitts (see page 21) and Footies makes a great birthday or holiday gift. Since they work up quickly, you can make a set for each member of the family.

Geometric Bags

The large bag is the perfect size for carrying a notebook or magazine, while the small bag features an appliquéd flower and is sized for carrying a wallet and some lipstick.

Finished Sizes
Large bag: 9" x 12"
Small bag: 6" x 6"

Materials
Yarn: 100% Superwash wool heavy worsted-weight yarn (4) in following amounts:

Large Bag
   A: 130 yds (plum)
   B: 65 yds (pink)
   C: 65 yds (orange)
   D: 65 yds (white)

Small Bag
   A: 130 yds (pink)
   B: 65 yds (plum)
   C: 65 yds (white)

Hook: Size I-9 (5.5 mm) crochet hook or size required to obtain gauge

Notions: Tapestry needle, snap (optional), sewing needle and thread

Gauge
17 sts and 17 rows = 4" in sc on size I-9 hook

Large Bag
Work through the following instructions to make the large bag.

Back
With A, ch 3. Work 3 sc in 2nd ch from hook, turn.
Row 1: Ch 1, sc in first st, work 3 sc in next st, sc in last st—5 sts. Turn.
Row 2: Ch 1, sc in next 2 sts, work 3 sc in next st, sc in next 2 sts—7 sts. Turn.
Row 3: Ch 1, sc in next 3 sts, work 3 sc in next st, sc in next 3 sts—9 sts. Turn.

Row 4: Ch 1, sc in next 4 sts, work 3 sc in next st, sc in next 4 sts—11 sts. Turn.
Cont in this manner, working 1 more sc before and after center inc st with each subsequent row until you've completed row 35.
Row 36: Ch 1, sc in next 36 sts, work 3 sc in next st, sc in next 36 sts—75 sts. Turn.
Row 37: Ch 1, sc in next 38 sts, turn.
Work last row 11 more times. On 12th row, do not turn at end of row and do not break yarn.
Edging: With A, sc down left selvage, along bottom, up right selvage, and across top, working 1 sc per st/row and working ch 1 at each corner. Join last sc to first sc with sl st. Break yarn and fasten off.

Front
With B, work as for back, working rows 1–12 with B, 13–24 with C, and 25–36 with D. Work 12 sc rows as for back, working rows 1–4 with B, 5–8 with C, and 9–12 with D. With A, work edging as for back.

Finishing
Block front and back pieces flat. With WS tog and A, sew pieces tog with an overcast seam. With sewing needle and thread, sew snap in place on inside of bag if desired.
Strap: With A, dbl ch (see "Double Chain" on page 9) to desired strap length plus 2". Keep in mind that strap will stretch when bag is carried, so measure both unstretched and stretched lengths. Straps on bags shown measure 32" unstretched. Ch 1, sc 1 row along dbl ch. Break yarn and fasten off. Block strap (it will be a bit curly when finished). Sew into place about 1" down along inside of bag.

Double Chain

The double-chain technique creates a base chain followed by a row of single crochet all in one shot, saving the step of having to work a row of single crochet on a long, snaky chain.

Chain two, insert hook in the second chain from the hook, yarn over, draw yarn through chain (two loops on hook), draw yarn through both loops. *Insert hook in left loop of single crochet just made, yarn over (fig. 1), draw yarn through the left loop only (two loops on hook; fig. 2), yarn over, draw yarn through both loops (fig. 3). Repeat from * for the desired number of chains.

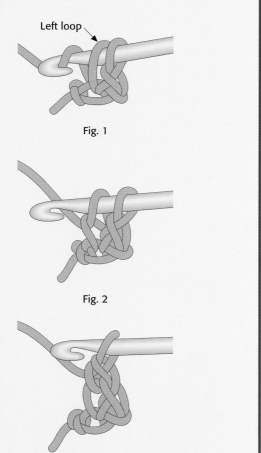

Left loop

Fig. 1

Fig. 2

Fig. 3

Small Bag

Work through the following instructions to make the small bag.

Back

With A, work as for large bag through row 24—51 sts. Work edging as for large bag.

Front

Work as for large bag through row 24—51 sts.
Break C.
With A, work edging as for large bag.

Finishing

Work as for large bag.
If desired, appliqué a flower to front of bag. Bag shown uses Simple Flower 2 with a contrasting-color Flower Center (page 32).

Retro Scarf

Built one block at a time, this colorful scarf can be modified to any length you like by simply adding or subtracting blocks.

Size

4½" x 54"

Materials

Yarn: 65 yds *each* of 5 colors of 100% Superwash wool* heavy worsted-weight yarn (4); label colors A, B, C, D, and E

Hook: Size K-10½ (6.5 mm) crochet hook or size required to obtain gauge

Notions: Tapestry needle

*Since the squares need to be blocked into shape, the pattern works best in wool.

Gauge

12 sts and 10 rows = 4" in hdc on size K-10½ hook

Basic Block

Finished block is approx 4½" x 4½" after blocking. Ch 2 at beg of rows does not count as a st.

Ch 3. Work 3 hdc in 3rd ch from hook, turn.

Row 1: Ch 2, hdc in first st, work 3 hdc in next st, hdc in last st, turn—5 sts.

Row 2: Ch 2, hdc in next 2 sts, work 3 hdc in next st, hdc in next 2 sts, turn—7 sts.

Row 3: Ch 2, hdc in next 3 sts, work 3 hdc in next st, hdc in next 3 sts, turn—9 sts.

Row 4: Ch 2, hdc in next 4 sts, work 3 hdc in next st, hdc in next 4 sts, turn—11 sts.

Row 5: Ch 2, hdc in next 5 sts, work 3 hdc in next st, hdc in next 5 sts, turn—13 sts.

Row 6: Ch 2, hdc in next 6 sts, work 3 hdc in next st, hdc in next 6 sts, turn—15 sts.

Row 7: Ch 2, hdc in next 7 sts, work 3 hdc in next st, hdc in next 7 sts, turn—17 sts.

Row 8: Ch 2, hdc in next 8 sts, work 3 hdc in next st, hdc in next 8 sts, turn—19 sts.

Row 9: Ch 2, hdc in next 9 sts, work 3 hdc in next st, hdc in next 9 sts, do not turn—21 sts.

Edging: Ch 1, work 9 hdc evenly along side selvage, ch 1, work 1 hdc in corner (where first 3 hdc of block were worked), ch 1, work 9 hdc along 2nd selvage, ch 1, join to top edge with sl st.

Break yarn, fasten off. Block piece into a flat square. Weave in ends.

Make 12 blocks in the following (or your own) color combinations. Work edging for each block in last color used (row 9).

Block 1
Rows 1–3: D
Rows 4–6: A
Rows 7–9: B

Block 2
Rows 1–3: A
Rows 4–6: B
Rows 7–9: C

Block 3
Rows 1–3: C
Rows 4–6: A
Rows 7–9: B

Block 4
Rows 1–3: C
Rows 4–6: B
Rows 7–9: A

Block 5
Rows 1–9: C

Block 6
Rows 1–3: B
Rows 4–6: C
Rows 7–9: A

Block 7
Rows 1–3: A
Rows 4–6: D
Rows 7–9: C

Block 8
Rows 1–9: B

Block 9
Rows 1–3: B
Rows 4–6: C
Rows 7–9: D

Block 10
Rows 1–3: A
Rows 4–6: C
Rows 7–9: B

Block 11
Rows 1–9: A

Block 12
Rows 1–3: B
Rows 4–6: A
Rows 7–9: D

Finishing

Sew blocks tog with an overcast seam, working into 10 sts from each block. Keep them in numerical order but rotate them in different directions to make design more interesting.

Edging: With D, and starting at lower corner of scarf, work blo sc around scarf edges, working 10 to 11 sc along each square and working 1 ch on either side of corner sts of scarf (not individual squares). Finish by joining last edge st to first edge st with sl st.

Break yarn and fasten off. Weave in ends. Even though individual squares have already been blocked, block scarf again once squares are joined.

Color-Block Scarves

Lightweight and soft, and with options for a subtle tonal palette or a flamboyant multicolored design, this scarf is sure to please.

Sizes
Child/Adult Short: 4" x 47"
Adult Medium: 4" x 56¼"
Adult Long: 4" x 75"

Materials
Yarn: 50% wool, 50% cotton blend DK-weight yarn (3) in following amounts:
Child/Adult Short: 118 yds *each* of 3 colors; label colors A, B, and C
Adult Medium: 60 yds *each* of 6 colors; label colors A–F
Adult Long: 236 yds *each* of 2 colors, A and C; 118 yds of color B
Hook: Size H-8 (5 mm) crochet hook or size required to obtain gauge
Notions: Tapestry needle

Gauge
23 sts and 11 rows = 4" in front-loop counterpane st on H-8 hook

Front-Loop Counterpane Stitch
All rows: Ch 2 (count as st), YO, insert hook in FL of second st, YO, draw lp through this st and first lp on hook, YO, draw through rem lps, *YO, insert hook in FL of next st, YO, draw lp through this st and first lp on hook, YO, draw through rem lps; rep from * across row, working last st in top of tch from previous row, turn.

Three-Color Scarf
Child/Adult Short (Adult Long)
With A, ch 25.
Row 1 (set-up row): YO, insert hook in third ch from hook, YO, draw lp through this ch and first lp on hook, YO, draw through rem lps, *YO, insert hook in next ch, YO, draw lp through this ch and first lp on hook, YO, draw through rem lps; rep from * across row—23 sts. Turn.

Work front-loop counterpane st for 11 more rows with A (first block made). Then, cont patt st throughout in color sequence as follows:
1 row with B
12 rows with C
1 row with B
12 rows with A
Rep color sequence until you've completed 10 (16) total blocks. Fasten off and weave in ends.

Six-Color Scarf
Work as given for Child/Adult Short (Adult Long) scarf, placing colors as follows:
12 rows with A (set-up row followed by 11 rows of front-loop counterpane st)
1 row with F
12 rows with B
1 row with A
12 rows with C
1 row with B
12 rows with D
1 row with C
12 rows with E
1 row with D
12 rows with F
1 row with E
12 rows with A
1 row with F
12 rows with B
1 row with A
12 rows with C
1 row with B
12 rows with D
1 row with C
12 rows with E
1 row with D
12 rows with F
Break yarn and fasten off. Weave in ends.

Ruffle-Edge Hat

Ruffles and easy embroidered accents add charm to this feminine design.

Sizes

To fit: 6 mos–1 yr (2–4 yrs, 5 yrs–Adult)
Circumference: 16¾ (19¼, 21½)"

Materials

Yarn: Wool-cotton blend DK-weight yarn **3** in following amounts:
  MC: 113 (113, 226) yds
  CC1: 113 yds (all sizes)
  CC2: Small amount for embroidery
Hook: Size H-8 (5 mm) crochet hook or size required to obtain gauge
Notions: Split-ring marker, tapestry needle

Gauge

20 sts and 22 rnds = 4" in sc with H-8 hook

Crown

With MC, ch 5, join into a ring with sl st.
Rnd 1: Work 6 sc in ring. Pm in last sc of rnd. Move marker to last sc with each subsequent rnd.
Rnd 2: Work 2 sc in next 6 sts—12 sts.
Rnd 3: *Sc in next st, work 2 sc in next st; rep from * around—18 sts.
Rnd 4: *Sc in next 2 sts, work 2 sc in next st; rep from * around—24 sts.
Rnd 5: *Sc in next 3 sts, work 2 sc in next st; rep from * around—30 sts.
Rnd 6: *Sc in next 4 sts, work 2 sc in next st; rep from * around—36 sts.
Rnd 7: *Sc in next 5 sts, work 2 sc in next st; rep from * around—42 sts.
Rnd 8: *Sc in next 6 sts, work 2 sc in next st; rep from * around—48 sts.

Rnd 9: *Sc in next 7 sts, work 2 sc in next st; rep from * around—54 sts.
Rnd 10: *Sc in next 8 sts, work 2 sc in next st; rep from * around—60 sts.
Cont in this manner, inc 6 sts per rnd, until you complete rnd 14 (16, 18). *Sc in next 12 (14, 16) sts, work 2 sc in next st; rep from * around—84 (96, 108) sts.
Work even in sc until hat measures 5 (5¾, 6½)" from start.
Change to CC1 and sc for 3 (3, 5) rnds. Break yarn.

Brim

With MC, sc 1 rnd.

For Six Months–One Year (Two–Four Years)

Rnd 1: *Sc in next 6 (7) sts, work 2 sc in next st; rep from * around—96 (108) sts.
Rnd 2: *Sc in next 7 (8) sts, work 2 sc in next st; rep from * around—108 (120) sts.
Rnd 3: Sc in next 4 (4) sts, work 2 sc in next st, *sc in next 8 (9) sts, work 2 sc in next st; rep from * around, end with sc in last 4 (5) sts—120 (132) sts.
Rnd 4: Sc in next 5 (5) sts, work 2 sc in next st, *sc in next 9 (10) sts, work 2 sc in next st; rep from * around, end with sc in last 4 (5) sts—132 (144) sts.
Sc 2 (2) rnds even. Finish last rnd by joining last st of rnd to first st of rnd with sl st. Break yarn and fasten off. Weave in ends.

For Five Years–Adult

Rnd 1: *Sc in next 8 sts, work 2 sc in next st; rep from * around—120 sts.
Rnd 2: *Sc in next 9 sts, work 2 sc in next st; rep from * around—132 sts.

Rnd 3: *Sc in next 10 sts, work 2 sc in next st; rep from * around—144 sts.

Rnd 4: Sc in next 5 sts, work 2 sc in next st, *sc in next 11 sts, work 2 sc in next st; rep from * around, end with sc in last 6 sts—156 sts.

Rnd 5: Sc in next 6 sts, work 2 sc in next st, *sc in next 12 sts, work 2 sc in next st; rep from * around, end with sc in last 6 sts—168 sts.

Rnd 6: Sc in next 7 sts, work 2 sc in next st, *sc in next 13 sts, work 2 sc in next st; rep from * around, end with sc in last 6 sts—180 sts.

Sc 3 rnds even. Finish last rnd by joining last st of rnd to first st of rnd with sl st. Break yarn and fasten off. Weave in ends.

Finishing

With CC2, embroider flowers along band just above brim as follows: Thread yarn through tapestry needle and *bring needle up from the wrong side at A and insert needle 2 sc sts away at B (fig. 1). Bring needle up at C and insert needle diagonally at D (just above B; fig. 2). Bring needle up at E and insert needle diagonally at F (just above A) to complete the flower (fig. 3). Make the next flower 1 sc away from previous flower. Rep from * around. Break yarn and fasten off. Weave in ends.

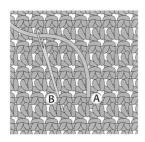

Fig. 1

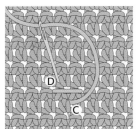

Fig. 2

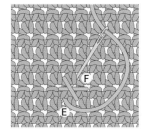

Fig. 3

Preemie Hats

Your local hospital may welcome a donation of preemie hats to keep newborns warm—and you'll get to use up leftover yarn. Win-win!

Size

Head circumference: From 4¾" to 14"

Materials

Yarn: Small amount of soft, machine-washable yarn of any sock (**1**), sport (**2**), DK (**3**), or worsted weight (**4**)

Hook: Size appropriate to yarn weight

Notions: Split-ring marker, tapestry needle

Gauge

This pattern allows you to make a single-crochet preemie hat using any yarn and hook you wish, without having to worry about gauge.

Directions

With yarn and appropriate-size hook, ch 2. Work 6 sc in 2nd ch from hook, pm in first sc worked, do not turn.

Rnd 1: Work 2 sc in marked st (this will join work into a circle), 2 sc in next 5 sts—12 sts. Pm in last st of rnd, then move marker to last st of each subsequent rnd.

Rnd 2: *Sc in next st, work 2 sc in next st; rep from * around—18 sts.

Rnd 3: *Sc in next 2 sts, work 2 sc in next st; rep from * around—24 sts.

Rnd 4: *Sc in next 3 sts, work 2 sc in next st; rep from * around—30 sts.

Cont in this manner, working 1 more sc before inc st with each subsequent row until hat measures diameter for desired circumference; see table on page 19.

Diameter	Approximate Circumference
1½"	4¾"
1¾"	5½"
2"	6¼"
2¼"	7"
2½"	7¾"
2¾"	8½"
3"	9½"
3¼"	10¼"
3½"	11"
3¾"	11¾"
4"	12½"
4¼"	13¼"
4½"	14"

Count number of inc rnds worked to this point, then work same number of rnds without inc. For example, if you worked 6 inc rnds, you will work 6 rnds even. This will give you a hat that ends approx just above ears. To make a hat that covers ears, work even number of rnds equal to 1½ times the number of inc rnds. On a hat with 6 inc rnds, you will work 9 rnds even for a hat that covers ears.

Note: You may need to adjust the number of rounds you work even to accommodate a pattern, such as on the striped hat shown. Not to worry—the hat will still fit some little sweetie!

Alternate Sizes

If you want to make a hat in a circumference that isn't listed in the chart at left, divide the desired circumference by 3.1416 to obtain the diameter you need. For example, if you need to make a hat with a 5" circumference: 5" ÷ 3.1416 = 1.59". Although 1.59" is a little difficult to measure, you know that the diameter needs to be a bit larger than 1½" and a bit less than 1¾".

Finishing

Weave in ends.

Embellish with crocheted flowers, if desired.

Note: When making hats for babies and young children, make sure to sew embellishments, such as the flower shown here, very securely. Use knots to finish the ends of the sewing yarn, since simple weaving may not be enough to keep little fingers from pulling the flower off. (Flower patterns are on pages 31 and 32.)

Fingerless Mitts

*Keep your hands warm while still being able
to use your fingers!*

Finished Sizes

To fit: Child Small (Child Medium/Adult Small, Adult
Medium, Adult Large)

Hand circumference: 5¾ (7, 8½, 10)"

Materials

Yarn: 100% merino wool worsted-weight yarn (4)
in following amounts:

MC: 175 yds

CC: Small amount

Hooks: Size 7 (4.5 mm) and size H-8 (5 mm) crochet
hooks or sizes required to obtain gauge

Notions: Split-ring marker, tapestry needle

Gauge

17 sts and 20 rnds = 4" in sc on larger hook

Cuff

With smaller hook and MC, ch 5 (6, 7, 7). Sc in 2nd ch
from hook and in each ch across, turn—4 (5, 6, 6) sts.
*Ch 1, sc in first st, flo sc in next 2 (3, 4, 4) sts, sc in
last st, turn.
Rep from * until you've worked 20 (26, 30, 36) rows
total.
Break yarn and fasten off. Seam short edges of
cuff tog.

Hand

Change to larger hook and starting at cuff seam, sc 20
(26, 30, 36) sts around top of cuff with MC. Pm in last
st of rnd. Sc 1 rnd.

Next rnd: Sc to last st, work 2 sc in last st—21 (27, 31,
37) sts.

Next rnd: Work 2 sc in first st, sc around—22 (28, 32,
38) sts.

Rep last 2 rnds 1 (1, 2, 2) more times—24 (30, 36,
42) sts.

Sc 3 (5, 5, 6) rnds even.

Thumb Opening

Next rnd: Ch 7 (8, 10, 11), sk next 5 (6, 7, 8) sts and sc
in 6th (7th, 8th, 9th) st, sc to end of rnd.

Next rnd: Sc across 7 (8, 10, 11) chs, sc to end of rnd.

Next rnd: (Sc2tog, 2 sc) 2 (2, 3, 3) times, sc to end of
rnd—24 (30, 36, 42) sts.

Work even for 4 (6, 8, 10) more rnds. Break yarn and
fasten off. Weave in ends.

Finishing

With MC, work 1 rnd sc along lower edge of cuff; then
with CC, work 1 rnd sc. Finish last rnd by joining last st
of rnd to first st of rnd with sl st. Break yarn and fasten
off. Weave in ends.

Classic Hat

*Work this classic crochet hat in a solid color
or playful stripes. Add an optional crochet flower
for a romantic touch.*

Sizes
To fit: 2 yrs (3–4 yrs, 5 yrs–Adult)
Circumference: 18½ (20, 21½)"

Materials
Yarn: Approx 205 yds of 100% mercerized cotton DK-
weight yarn (**3**) for single-color hat; approx 70 yds
each of 3 colors for striped hat
Hook: Size H-8 (5 mm) crochet hook or size required
to obtain gauge
Notions: Split-ring marker, tapestry needle, small
amounts of additional colors for flower embellish-
ment (optional)

Gauge
18 sts and 20 rnds = 4" in sc on size H-8 hook

Single-Color Hat
Ch 2. Work 6 sc in 2nd ch from hook, pm in first sc
worked, do not turn.
Rnd 1: Work 2 sc in marked st (this will join work into
a circle), 2 sc in next 5 sts—12 sts. Pm in last st of rnd,
then move marker to last st of each subsequent rnd.
Rnd 2: *Sc in next st, work 2 sc in next st; rep from *
around—18 sts.
Rnd 3: *Sc in next 2 sts, work 2 sc in next st; rep from
* around—24 sts.
Rnd 4: *Sc in next 3 sts, work 2 sc in next st; rep from
* around—30 sts.
Rnd 5: *Sc in next 4 sts, work 2 sc in next st; rep from
* around—36 sts.
Rnd 6: *Sc in next 5 sts, work 2 sc in next st; rep from
* around—42 sts.
Rnd 7: *Sc in next 6 sts, work 2 sc in next st; rep from
* around—48 sts.
Rnd 8: *Sc in next 7 sts, work 2 sc in next st; rep from
* around—54 sts.
Rnd 9: *Sc in next 8 sts, work 2 sc in next st; rep from
* around—60 sts.
Rnd 10: *Sc in next 9 sts, work 2 sc in next st; rep from
* around—66 sts.

Rnd 11: *Sc in next 10 sts, work 2 sc in next st; rep from *
around—72 sts.
Rnd 12: *Sc in next 11 sts, work 2 sc in next st; rep from *
around—78 sts.
Rnd 13: *Sc in next 12 sts, work 2 sc in next st; rep
from * around—84 sts. (Size 2 yrs, skip to ** below)
Rnd 14: *Sc in next 13 sts, work 2 sc in next st; rep
from * around—90 sts. (Size 3–4 yrs, skip to ** below).
Rnd 15: *Sc in next 14 sts, work 2 sc in next st; rep
from * around—96 sts. (Size 5 yrs–Adult, go to ** below).
**Cont in sc without inc until hat measures 6½ (7, 7½)"
from start, moving marker to last st of every rnd.
Work 1 rnd blo sc, join last st of rnd to first st of rnd
with sl st. Break yarn and fasten off. Weave in ends.
Optional: Make flower or flowers of your choice (pages
31 and 32) and sew to hat. Hat shown features a two-
tone Spiral Flower.

Striped Hat
Label yarns A, B, and C.
Starting with A, work as for single-color hat through
rnd 2.
Rnd 3: Beg stripe patt while cont shaping as for single-
color hat.

Stripe Pattern
Do not break yarns between rnds; carry them up
inside of work. Work stripe patt as follows:
    2 rnds with B
    1 rnd with A
    2 rnds with C
    1 rnd with A
Rep stripe-patt sequence for length of hat, ending
with a completed stripe B or C (the color you end with
will vary with the size you're making). Break both B
and C.
With A, work 1 rnd sc. Then work 1 rnd blo sc, join last
st of rnd to first st of rnd with sl st. Break yarn and
fasten off. Weave in ends.

Pretty Pink Hat and Scarf

Elegant and easy to make, this hat looks great on babies, children, and adults. A simple pattern creates the coordinating all-season scarf.

Sizes

Scarf: 4" x 53"

Hat

> To fit: 6 mos–1 yr (2–4 yrs, 5 yrs–Adult)
> Circumference: 17 (18¾, 20½)"

Note: This combination of yarn and stitch pattern creates a stretchy fabric. The hat fits snugly and will accommodate a range of head sizes.

Materials

Yarn: Approx 87 yds of cotton/cashmere blend DK-weight yarn (3) for hat; approx 175 yds for scarf

Hook: Size I-9 (5.5 mm) crochet hook or size required to obtain gauge

Notions: Split-ring marker, tapestry needle

Gauge

Hat: 14 sts and 10 rnds = 4" in crossed half double crochet on size I-9 hook

Scarf: 18 sts and 9 rows = 4" in patt on I-9 hook

Crossed Half Double Crochet Stitch

Worked in the rnd.

All rnds: Ch 2 (count as st), *sk next st, hdc in next st, hdc in previously skipped st; rep from * around, end with hdc, join with sl st in top of beg ch.

> ### Find the Skips
> To help you find the skipped stitch when working crossed half double crochet, put a marker in it.

Hat

Ch 3 at beg of rnd counts as a st.

Ch 5 and join into ring with sl st.

Rnd 1: Ch 3, work 11 dc in ring, sl st in top of beg ch—12 sts.

Rnd 2: Ch 3, dc in base of ch, work 2 dc in next 11 sts, sl st in top of beg ch—24 sts.

Rnd 3: Ch 3, work 2 dc in next st, (dc in next st, work 2 dc in next st) 11 times, sl st in top of tch—36 sts.

Rnd 4: Ch 3, dc in next st, work 2 dc in next st, (dc in next 2 sts, work 2 dc in next st) 11 times, sl st in top of beg ch—48 sts.

Rnd 5: Ch 3, dc in next 2 sts, work 2 dc in next st, (dc in next 3 sts, work 2 dc in next st) 11 times, sl st in top of beg ch—60 sts.

For Six Months–One Year

Skip to ** below.

For Two–Four Years

Rnd 6: Ch 3, dc in next 8 sts, work 2 dc in next st, (dc in next 9 sts, work 2 dc in next st) 5 times, sl st in top of beg ch—66 sts. Skip to ** below.

For Five Years–Adult

Rnd 6: Ch 3, dc in next 3 sts, work 2 dc in next st, (dc in next 4 sts, work 2 dc in next st) 11 times, sl st in top of beg ch—72 sts. Go to ** below.

**Work in crossed half double crochet for 5 (6, 9) rnds.

Next rnd: Ch 1, sc around, join last sc to first sc with a sl st. Break yarn and fasten off. Weave in ends.

Scarf

Ch 19, sc in 2nd ch from hook and in each ch across—18 sts; turn.

Set-up row: Ch 2 (count as st), sk first st, *sk next st, hdc in next st, hdc in skipped st; rep from * across, turn.

Row 1: Ch 3 (count as st), sk first st, *work 2 dc in next st, sk next st; rep from * across, end with dc in top of tch, turn.

Row 2: Ch 2 (count as st), sk first st, *sk next st, hdc in next st, hdc in skipped st; rep from * across, end with hdc in top of tch, turn.

Rep rows 1 and 2 until scarf is 53" long, ending with completed row 2.

Last row: Ch 1, sc in first st (base of tch), sc in next 17 sts (do not sc in tch from previous row). Break yarn and fasten off. Weave in ends.

Booties

Simple and sweet, these booties will keep Baby's toes warm and cozy. The colorful ribbon helps the booties stay put.

Size
Foot circumference: 4"
Foot length: 2½"

Materials
Yarn: Approx 87 yds of cotton-cashmere blend DK-weight yarn (**3**)
Hook: Size H-8 (5 mm) crochet hook or size required to obtain gauge
Notions: Split-ring marker, tapestry needle, 1 yd of ribbon (⅜" wide)

Gauge
18 sts and 20 rows = 4" in sc on size H-8 hook

Different-Sized Booties?
Simply follow the directions as written, using a finer yarn and smaller hook for a smaller bootie, or a bulkier yarn and larger hook for a bigger bootie.

Foot
Ch 2. Work 6 sc in 2nd ch from hook, pm in first sc worked, do not turn.
Rnd 1: Work 2 sc in marked st (this will join work into a circle), 2 sc in next 5 sts—12 sts. Pm in last st of rnd, then move marker to last st of each subsequent rnd.
Rnd 2: *Sc in next 5 sts, work 2 sc in next st; rep from * around—14 sts.
Rnd 3: *Sc in next 6 sts, work 2 sc in next st; rep from * around—16 sts.
Rnd 4: *Sc in next 7 sts, work 2 sc in next st; rep from * around—18 sts.
Sc 5 rnds even.

Heel
Sc in first st, turn, remove marker.
(Ch 1, sc in next 14 sts, turn) 2 times.
Ch 1, sc in next 4 sts, sc2tog 3 times, sc in last 4 sts, turn—11 sts.
Ch 1, sc in next 11 sts, turn.
Ch 1, sc in next 4 sts, sc3tog, sc in last 4 sts, turn—9 sts.
Ch 1, sc in next 9 sts. Break yarn and fasten off.

Finishing
Sew center-back heel seam. Then attach yarn at center-back heel and sc 2 rows around foot opening. Finish last rnd by joining last st of rnd to first st of rnd with a sl st. Break yarn and fasten off. Weave in ends. Cut ribbon into two 18" lengths. Thread through tapestry needle and weave in and out of spaces between stitches around foot opening. Trim ribbon to desired length. To keep ribbon from slipping out of booties, tack each ribbon into place at back of heel with a sewing needle and thread.

Options and Tips for Making the Booties

- Grosgrain ribbon is another pretty option, and it's less slippery than satin ribbon.

- Because they require so little yarn, booties are a great way to use up the odds and ends of stash yarn. Just be sure to adjust your hook size to the weight of the yarn you're using.

- Colorful take-out containers, available at many paper, craft, and party-supply stores, are a fun a way to package the booties for gift giving.

- Premature babies need booties to warm their tiny tootsies. Why not make several pairs to give to your local hospital's preemie ward? If you'd like to help some little one stay cozy from head to toe, see page 17 for instructions on making no-gauge preemie hats.

Sweet Baby Hat

Here's a baby gift you can crochet in just a few hours. The soft yarn and vivid, pretty colors make this hat a sure winner.

Sizes
To fit: 0–6 mos (1 yr, 2 yrs, 3–4 yrs)
Circumference: 15½ (17, 18¾, 20½)"

Materials
Yarn: Approx 90 yds *each* of 2 colors of cotton-acrylic microfiber blend worsted-weight yarn (4); label yarns A and B*
Hook: Size J-10 (6 mm) crochet hook or size needed to obtain gauge
Notions: Split-ring marker, tapestry needle

*Ninety yds of each color is enough to make two hats, as long as you reverse the color placement. See the tip box below right if you'd like to make a multicolored hat.

Gauge
14 sts and 16 rnds = 4" in sc on J-10 hook

Directions
The crown of this hat is worked in a spiral.
With A, ch 2. Work 6 sc in 2nd ch from hook, pm in first sc worked, do not turn.
Rnd 1: Work 2 sc in marked st (this will join work into a circle), 2 sc in next 5 sts—12 sts. Pm in last st of rnd, then move marker to last st of each subsequent rnd.
Rnd 2: *Sc in next st, work 2 sc in next st; rep from * around—18 sts.
Rnd 3: *Sc in next 2 sts, work 2 sc in next st; rep from * around—24 sts.

Rnd 4: *Sc in next 3 sts, work 2 sc in next st; rep from * around—30 sts.
Rnd 5: *Sc in next 4 sts, work 2 sc in next st; rep from * around—36 sts.
Rnd 6: *Sc in next 5 sts, work 2 sc in next st; rep from * around—42 sts.
Rnd 7: *Sc in next 6 sts, work 2 sc in next st; rep from * around—48 sts.
Rnd 8: *Sc in next 7 sts, work 2 sc in next st; rep from * around—54 sts. (Size 0–6 mos, skip to ** below.)
Rnd 9: *Sc in next 8 sts, work 2 sc in next st; rep from * around—60 sts. (Size 1 yr, skip to ** below.)
Rnd 10: *Sc in next 9 sts, work 2 sc in next st; rep from * around—66 sts. (Size 2 yrs, skip to ** below.)
Rnd 11: *Sc in next 10 sts, work 2 sc in next st; rep from * around—72 sts. (Size 3–4 yrs, go to ** below.)
**All sizes: With B, sc for 12 rnds without inc. With A, sc 1 rnd. Join last st of rnd to first st of rnd with a sl st. Break yarn and fasten off.

> ### Multicolor Hat
> After working the crown (rounds 1–11), change colors and work three rounds. Work nine more rounds, changing colors after every three rounds. With A, single crochet one round and finish as for two-color hat.

From top to bottom, Simple Flower with Flower Center, Spiral Flower, Clover Leaves

Floral Wristbands and Choker

Brighten up your wardrobe with these colorful flowered bands.

Finished Sizes

To fit: Child (Adult)
Wrist Bands: 6½ (7½)" long, unbuttoned
Choker: 13½ (14½)" long, unbuttoned

Note: You'll lose about 1" in circumference once the bands are buttoned. Length can be adjusted by starting with extra chains for a longer band or fewer chains for a shorter band.

Materials

Yarn: Small amounts of 100% mercerized cotton DK-weight yarn **❸** in a variety of colors
Hook: Size 7 (4.5 mm) crochet hook or size required to obtain gauge
Notions: Tapestry needle, button(s) (⅜" to ½" diameter), sewing thread and needle

Gauge

18 sts and 20 rows = 4" in sc on size 7 hook

Basic Cuff

With desired color, ch 31 (35). Sc in 2nd ch from hook and in each ch across—30 (34) sts, turn.
Rows 1, 2, 4, and 5: Ch 1, sc in next 30 (34) sts, turn.
Row 3 (buttonhole row): Ch 1, sc in next 2 sts, ch 2, sk 2 sts, sc to end of row, turn.
Break yarn and fasten off.

> ### Buttonhole Tip
> It's perfectly fine to single crochet under the front loop only of the buttonhole chain if this is easier for you than working under the entire chain.

Block cuff so it lies flat. Sew button(s) to cuff to correspond with buttonhole(s). Make flowers as desired (see flower instructions at right) and sew to cuff. Use knots to secure your sewing yarn.

Wide Cuff

With desired color, ch 31 (35). Sc in 2nd ch from hook and in each ch across—30 (34) sts, turn.
Rows 1, 2, 4, 5, and 6: Ch 1, sc in next 30 (34) sts, turn.
Row 3 (buttonhole row): Ch 1, sc in next 2 sts, ch 2, sk 2 sts, sc to end of row, turn.
Rep rows 3–6 until cuff is desired width, ending after completing row 5 on final rep.
Break yarn and fasten off. Finish as for basic cuff.

Choker

With desired color, ch 62 (66). Sc in 2nd ch from hook and in each ch across—61 (65) sts, turn.
Rows 1, 2, 4, and 5: Ch 1, sc in next 61 (65) sts, turn.
Row 3 (buttonhole row): Ch 1, sc in next 2 sts, ch 2, sk 2 sts, sc to end of row, turn.
Break yarn and fasten off. Finish as for basic cuff.

Flowers

Simple Flower 1 (chartreuse) and Simple Flower 2 (coral)

Materials

You'll need small amounts of DK-weight yarn in a variety of colors to coordinate with your project, size 7 (4.5 mm) crochet hook, and tapestry needle

Gauge

18 sts and 20 rows = 4" in sc on size 7 hook

Simple Flower 1

Ch 5, join into ring with sl st.

Ch 3, work 9 dc in ring, join last dc to top of ch with sl st—10 sts.

*Ch 2, work 2 dc in next st, ch 2, sl st in next st; rep from * around.

Break yarn and fasten off.

Simple Flower 2

This flower has bigger petals and a more open center than Simple Flower 1.

Ch 6, join in ring with sl st.

Ch 1, work 15 sc in ring, joining last sc to first sc with sl st—15 sts.

*Ch 3, dc2tog in next st 2 times, ch 3, sl st in next st; rep from * around.

Break yarn and fasten off.

Flower Center

Ch 4. Sk first ch, sc in next 3 ch. Break yarn.

Sew short ends of fabric tog. You don't have to do this perfectly; you're just making a ball shape to fill in the hole created by the starting ring of the flower.

To make a larger center, make a longer starting ch, sk first ch, sc in rem ch.

Combo Flower

Make a Simple Flower 1 or Simple Flower 2, one Two-Tone Flower, and one Flower Center. Sew Two-Tone Flower onto Simple Flower; tack Flower Center in center opening.

Clover Leaves

Ch 4, join into ring with sl st.

Ch 1, work 6 sc in ring, join last sc to first sc with sl st—6 sts.

*Ch 2, work 2 dc in next st, ch 2, sl st in next st; rep from * around.

Break yarn and fasten off.

Spiral Flowers and Leaves

To make a Spiral Flower, make ch of any length, and then work 4 dc into each chain. This will give you a narrow, spiraling piece of fabric. To form flower, start at one end of spiral and coil fabric around itself, working in a free-form manner. An irregular, asymmetrical shape is more interesting and natural looking. Once you've formed your flower, use tapestry needle threaded with yarn to tack the spiral into place, sewing "petals" together as needed for flower to hold its shape and working as close to center of flower as possible. Complex motifs involving multiple flowers and leaves may be sewn to crinoline (available at fabric stores) before being sewn to the final garment. To make Leaves, use green yarn and construct as for Spiral Flower, but rather than coiling it around itself, arrange it behind your flower motif so that it looks like greenery.

Basic spiral flower. Ch 24. Work 3 dc in 4th ch from hook. Work 4 dc in each of next 20 chs. Break yarn and fasten off. Form spiral into flower shape.

Two-tone spiral flower. With color 1, ch 24. Work 3 dc in 4th ch from hook, 4 dc in each of next 6 chs. Change to color 2 and work 4 dc in each rem ch. Break yarn and fasten off. Form spiral into flower shape.

For a larger flower, start with a longer chain. Large spiral flowers shown started with 48-st ch. To make the flower two tone, work ch and first ⅓ of ch sts in one color, and rem ⅔ of ch sts in another color. For small leaf accent, start with a chain of about 10 sts.

Spiral Flowers and Leaves